How to Be a Good Husband

A Classic Guide, Updated for Today

Brilliant (and Sometimes Questionable) Advice from the 1930s, Translated for Modern Life

Annotated by Rick Resnick

The Husband School

THE HUSBAND SCHOOL® PRESENTS:
How to Be a Good Husband: A Classic Guide, Updated for Today

© 2025 Rick Resnick

New editorial content, including the introduction, chapter introductions, annotations, and conclusion

The original text of *Do's and Don'ts for Husbands* (1936) is in the public domain in the United Kingdom and the United States. No claim is made to the original public-domain text.

All rights are reserved for the new editorial content in this edition. No part of this original editorial material may be reproduced or transmitted in any form or by any means without prior written permission from the publisher, except for brief quotations in reviews. For further information, please visit husbandschool.co/contact

This book is intended for general informational and entertainment purposes only and does not constitute professional, legal, financial, or medical advice. Readers should consult appropriate professionals for guidance specific to their situation. The author and publisher disclaim any liability arising from the use of the information contained in this work.

Note on Authorship and Editorial Process

This book was developed with the support of modern AI writing and research tools under the author's full creative direction. All final editorial content reflects the author's voice and judgment.

First paperback edition: February 2026

First ebook edition: February 2026

ISBN 979-8-9912429-4-3 (paperback)

ISBN 979-8-9912429-5-0 (ebook)

The Husband School is a division of U.S. Explorers, LLC.

A Note on the Text and Annotations

How to Be a Good Husband was originally published in the United Kingdom in 1936 under the title *Do's and Don'ts for Husbands*. The original text is in the public domain in the United Kingdom and the United States.

This edition has been newly prepared by The Husband School and includes substantial contemporary material created for modern readers. In addition to the complete original text, this edition features:

- A new book introduction and book conclusion
- New introductions to each chapter
- Over 80 exclusive annotations and editorial notes

The annotations are clearly marked using a five-icon system designed to provide context, translation, and perspective on the original advice:

✓ Timeless Advice

➜ Ahead of Its Time

ϕ Vintage Point of View

◆ Hidden Gem

ⓘ Modern Translation

All annotations and supplemental editorial content in this edition were created specifically for this publication.

Contents

Introduction from The Husband School	7
Dedication	15
1. From One Husband to Another	16
2. Personal Relations	24
3. Conversation	31
4. Personal Habits	36
5. Dress and Clothing	43
6. Finance	49
7. Health	55
8. Children	60
9. Recreations	67
10. Out and About	74
11. Entertaining	81
12. Theatres, Dinners, and Restaurants	85
13. General	89
Closing Thoughts from The Husband School	95
About the Author	99
Thank You for Reading	100

Introduction from The Husband School

Why a 1930s Marriage Manual from England Still Matters Today

In 1936, the world looked very different. There were no smartphones, no shared Google calendars, and no arguments about whose turn it was to unload the dishwasher—because, almost certainly, the wife *was* the dishwasher.

England was between wars, men wore hats as a matter of policy, and a large share of marriage advice came via religious institutions and teachings.

And yet, here we are, reading a small marriage manual from nearly a century ago. Why?

Because, despite the massive cultural shifts, technological leaps, and the evolution of the two-income household (which alone changed marriage forever), the core problems this book addresses feel oddly familiar. Husbands still do dumb things. Wives don't appreciate it.

Small misunderstandings still turn into big resentments, and the repeated defense of "I didn't mean anything by it" eventually wears thin.

How to Be a Good Husband was written for an emerging professional class of men whose social status was somewhere between the guys toiling in the mines and the aristocratic gentlemen inheriting the big bucks. These were men who wanted to be decent husbands, but weren't entirely sure how.

That alone gives the book's many "do's and don'ts" their staying power. Strip away the monocles, the motorcycles, and the crested blazers, and what's left is a surprisingly clear-eyed look at how marriages actually succeed or fail. Not in grand moments, but in daily behavior.

Marriage, it turns out, hasn't changed nearly as much as the technology has.

What This Book Is—and What It Isn't

Let's get one thing out of the way early. This is not a rulebook. It is not a sermon. And it is definitely not a demand that you live your life exactly as an enlightened British gent might have in the mid-1930s.

This book is a collection of observations. Practical ones. Occasionally, bossy ones. Sometimes charming, sometimes blunt, and occasionally so specific that you may wonder what, exactly, happened to the author that week.

It is also not a joke book, though it is often funny— intentionally and otherwise. We've resisted the urge to treat it like a novelty item because the original author was sincere. He cared deeply about marriage. (We are *presuming* "he" is a he. The author is uncredited and unknown.) He believed husbands had responsibilities beyond earning money and staying out of trouble.

And he assumed, radically for his time, that how a man behaved at home mattered more than how he acted in public.

You are not required to agree with everything in these pages. In fact, you shouldn't. Part of the value of reading a book like this today is noticing what you agree with, what makes you bristle, and what you might actually want to try.

Read it as a conversation across time, not a mandate.

THE SURPRISING MIX YOU'LL FIND INSIDE

If you're expecting wall-to-wall outdated attitudes, you'll be surprised.

Yes, some moments are unmistakably vintage. You will encounter strong feelings about hats, punctuality, not using a comb in public, and not splashing pedestrians with your car. You will discover advice that assumes a household structure very different from today's norms.

But threaded through all of that are insights that feel remarkably modern.

The author worries about husbands being emotionally absent long before the phrase existed. He understands how undermining your spouse in front of children damages more than authority. He even encourages fathers to be overtly enthusiastic about their daughters' new dolls.

Again and again, the book returns to the same idea: character shows up at home first. Kindness counts most where it's least visible. And conversely, small, thoughtless actions can undo many good intentions.

You'll find moments of genuine warmth, unexpected empathy, and the occasional line so *au courant* in its thinking you'll forget it was written in 1936.

HOW TO READ THIS BOOK (THE ANNOTATION KEY)

To help bridge the 90-year gap between then and now, we've added a few brief footnotes after each chapter. These aren't here to judge the past or rewrite it. They're here to help you read with context, clarity, and—when appropriate—a raised eyebrow.

You'll see five simple markers:

✓ Timeless Advice: Guidance that still holds up beautifully, with little or no translation required.

→ Ahead of Its Time: Ideas that feel surprisingly progressive, empathetic, or modern for their era.

⌽ Vintage POV: Advice that reflects the norms of its era. Interesting, sometimes useful, sometimes just revealing.

◆ Hidden Gem: A line or idea that might be easy to overlook but deserves a second glance.

ⓘ Modern Translation: A quick explanation when the language, reference, or custom might need decoding.

The notes are meant to add texture and perspective, not get in the way of the original text. You're free to ignore them, disagree with them, or argue with them in your head. That, too, is part of the experience.

A Classic, Reimagined

We see the repackaged and annotated *How to Be a Good Husband* as an older, more buttoned-up companion to *The New Husband's Survival Guide*—the tongue-in-cheek manual for 21st-century guys trying to peacefully cohabitate with a woman.

The latter book, published by The Husband School in 2025, has been discovered by many readers in the U.S. and U.K. who first stumbled upon an unaltered, word-for-word reprint of *How to Be a Good Husband*. Their online search then pointed them our way.

Which got us thinking.

If people are already reading these books together—one

Introduction from The Husband School

earnest and classic, one playful and modern—why not give the older one a gentle Husband School makeover?

This repackaged edition exists because the original deserved a little sprucing up and some context to help it sit more comfortably on a contemporary coffee table. Not to modernize it into something it isn't, but to let its best ideas shine more clearly and its stranger ones be read with good humor.

Our hope is simple: that you'll dive in, laugh occasionally, nod more often than you expect, and maybe try a few small nuggets of advice. You don't need to adopt the whole philosophy. You don't need to become a model husband overnight.

But you should probably pay closer attention to the small things, like toothpaste etiquette, chocolate candy purchases, and breakfast-time smiles. Because—according to *How to Be a Good Husband*—that's where a marriage is actually built.

How to Be a Good Husband

Dedication

TO HUSBANDS

The part which a husband must play in life is not exactly an easy one. He has definite obligations and numerous restrictions. Often, he will be puzzled as to why things have gone wrong.

This small volume of Do's and Don'ts should help to guide him away from errors and pitfalls, since it epitomizes the correct conduct of husbands.

I
From One Husband to Another

THE HUSBAND SCHOOL OVERVIEW:

This opening chapter sets the tone for everything that follows—frank, practical advice from someone who has clearly learned a few things the hard way. It covers the emotional basics of marriage: attention, honesty, humility, and the daily choice not to act like you're running your own personal kingdom. Some of the pre-WWII language shows its age, but the instincts underneath it feel strikingly current: stay connected, own your mistakes, and don't confuse authority with partnership. And don't celebrate when your mother-in-law finally leaves. At its core, this chapter is about how marriages actually work day to day—not in grand gestures, but in small, repeated choices. It's a solid place to start, and a useful one to come back to.

Don't lose sight of the fact that, once a man is married, the only sensible thing for him to do is to make the best of the circumstances. If his wife has faults, he should try to shut his eyes to them. It may be that he is not entirely perfect.

Don't allow yourself to grow indifferent to your wife. You once thought she was everything in the world, and she is still the same person. A little encouragement from you will generally act like magic and draw you both together again.

Of course, you must not expect your wife to be perfect. There are no perfect wives and no perfect husbands. And even perfection would be a little tiring, if it did exist. So don't brood over the fact that your wife has her faults.

Don't act the lord and master to your wife. You may be both of these to her, but even if you are, no wife wants the fact rammed down her throat. Even if she wants you to be her lord and master, she would rather you called it co-partnership. →

If you want your wife to be a real companion to you and take an interest in all you do, don't keep her in the dark about things. Tell her where you go, what you have seen, and what you did. ◆ If she begins to feel that she must mind her own business, you will gradually drift apart.

Don't be the type of husband who has no time for his wife. If you work all day and dash off somewhere at night by yourself, she will eat her heart out and, when it is all consumed, you will be just the one to cry out about her departed love. Make some of her recreations yours, and then you will be able to spend some of your leisure together.

No wife looks at everything from the same point of view as her husband does. She has her own point of view, and the husband has his. So, if you know a thing is black, don't be surprised if your wife says it is white. At any rate, don't fly into a rage because she is so silly. Just agree to differ.

Don't tell your wife terminological inexactitudes, which are, in plain English, lies. ⓘ A woman has a wonderful intuition for spotting even minor departures from the truth, and however much she has an aptitude for indulging in them herself, she scorns the male who utters them. Lying to her is a sign of weakness and weakness in a man she regards as a crime.

Don't let your wife get the impression that you feel superior because you earn the money. If this idea grows on her, she will regard you as a cad. After all, it is just as important in this world to know how to cook as to work at an office desk. ➜ And running a home is not all honey: it can be fairly puzzling at times. Therefore, if your wife can cook and sew, take your hat off to her.

And while talking of money, tell your wife all about your finances and don't hide the figures from her. We once knew a man who would never tell his wife how much he earned, and the silly fellow was always complaining that she never helped him to save. How could she help him when she was never allowed to know just where he stood?

Don't be a fault-finding husband. Of course, faults have to be pointed out at times, because after all, no wife is absolutely perfect. A blind-eye is very useful on most occasions, but when you really must mention some defect, choose your time judiciously. If your wife has had a tiring day, leave the "curtain-lecture" for another time.

If you have a temper—and most of us have something of the sort—tell your wife when you feel irritable. ◆ If she is wise, she will do one of two things: she will either give you a wide berth or she will humor you. The first deprives you of the opportunity of venting your feelings, and the second reveals to you what a gem of a wife you have. Above all, tell her when you are bad-tempered and don't leave her to find it out.

If your wife becomes dowdy, don't blame her. She would not dare to wear "anything" if you were the kind of husband who had always made a point of telling her when she looked nice. In her mind, she argues that you never notice what she wears, so what does it matter?

Don't tell your wife that you love her dearly, and then treat her as though she were dirt. ✓ She would much prefer you to say nothing and express your admiration by actions. Of course, most wives don't object to being told the fact if all the actions go to support it. Even then, they don't want to hear about it too often.

Things have got to a pretty bad pitch if a wife's eyes do not sparkle when her husband brings her home some unexpected trifle. So don't forget, a bunch of flowers, a box of sweets, a bottle of scent, or something quite personal, every now and again.

Don't be afraid of admitting the fact when you are wrong. If you go to your wife and say to her, "I was in the wrong, yesterday evening, I'm sorry," she will look up to you as a strong man. ✓ And that means a lot to a woman.

Don't try to regulate your wife's friends. Give her the credit of being able to choose them sensibly—even though some of them belong to your own sex. If you put your foot, it will only make her angry and then determined. And that is the sure road to open warfare.

Don't be a husband who treats his wife coarsely. Most women have a much greater regard for refinement than men have, and lapses in this direction are bound to give them an unpleasant shock.

Don't be a musty sort of fellow with nothing bright and fresh in your outlook. It must be a dreadful blow to a woman who pictures her husband as a knight in shining armour to have to realise that he is a dull sort of individual without aims and ambitions. Work up an enthusiasm for something in which your wife can take an interest. That will help you both.

Relations are often the cause of a good deal of dissension, and you must exercise all the wisdom of Solomon, and more, in approaching the "in-law" problems.

Don't, for instance, be like a bear with a sore head when your wife's mother arrives on the scene and, then, expect your wife to be all smiles when it's your own mother's turn to visit you. Your mother may be a hundred times as nice as her mother, but will your wife be able to see it?

And when your mother-in-law departs, and your wife gives a sigh of relief, don't duplicate the expression of relief. Be absolutely passive for, while your wife may cast stones at her own people, she will thoroughly resent it if you take a hand at the game, also. It is a privilege of hers, not yours.

Then, there are your own people to think about. Your sisters, for instance, may be absolutely charming. If they are, let your wife find that out for herself. Don't tell her that they possess all the virtues and, certainly, don't ram the fact down her throat. If you do, she will grow to hate them, and it will be largely your own fault.

Don't grumble because your wife insists on going over, with you, all the little trivialities of the past day. You may be tired and don't want to be bothered with what the butcher boy did or what the neighbour said. But look at it from the wife's point of view. If that is all she has to think about, it is high time you took her to the pictures or the theatre and gave her something to fill her mind.

And, lastly, if you are wondering which is the better, a car in the garage or a kiddie in the cot, don't hesitate to choose the latter. The car may appeal to you no end; but for a real purpose in life, the kiddie will beat it all hollow.

Notes from The Husband School:

→ Ahead of Its Time
"...she would rather you called it co-partnership."

This line clearly tries to pivot away from the phrase "lord and master," and with good reason. Beneath the dated phrasing is a surprisingly modern insight: marriages work better when nobody's issuing commands like they're running a small medieval fiefdom. "Co-partnership" may sound like a law firm, but it turns out to be a much better way to run a marriage.

◆ Hidden Gem
"Tell her where you go, what you have seen, and what you did."

This isn't a request for a travel itinerary; it's an invitation to stay connected. Sharing the small, boring details of your day is how two lives stay intertwined. Mystery may be romantic, but it's a terrible long-term communication strategy.

ⓘ Modern Translation
"Don't tell your wife terminological inexactitudes..."

This is 1930s British for "don't lie," delivered with a monocle and a raised eyebrow. The point, however, is blunt: technical truths, strategic omissions, and clever wordplay still count as dishonesty. And they are rarely as effective as the person using them thinks.

→ Ahead of Its Time
"...it is just as important... to know how to cook as to work at an office desk."

For a book published when men wore hats indoors, this is refreshingly sane. The author recognizes that running a household requires real skill, patience, and endurance—not just a cheerful attitude. In other words, this isn't "helping out." It's work. Real work.

◆ Hidden Gem
"If you have a temper… tell your wife when you feel irritable."

This is quietly sensible advice, the kind that prevents problems before they start. Announcing "I'm in a mood" is far kinder than making your partner reverse-engineer it from tone, silence, or slammed cupboards. A warning label saves a lot of unnecessary damage.

✓ Timeless Advice
"Don't tell your wife that you love her dearly, and then treat her as though she were dirt."

Blunt, yes, but hard to improve on. Love that exists only in words, birthday cards, or anniversary flowers doesn't hold much weight for long. Affection that isn't backed up by behavior quickly stops meaning much. Romance survives on follow-through.

✓ Timeless Advice
"If you go to your wife and say… 'I was in the wrong… I'm sorry,' she will look up to you as a strong man."

This is one of marriage's greatest cheat codes. A sincere apology doesn't make you smaller; it makes the argument end faster. You don't lose authority by admitting fault. You just save everyone the trouble of a few exhausting follow-up conversations.

⊕ Vintage POV
"And when your mother-in-law departs ... don't duplicate the expression of relief."

The social choreography here belongs to another era, but the core advice is evergreen: Stay neutral, resist commentary, and choose your words (and facial expressions) carefully. Family politics reward silence far more often than clever remarks.

II
Personal Relations

THE HUSBAND SCHOOL OVERVIEW:

The author tackles how you behave when the door is closed and the audience is gone. He covers tone, timing, and the small decisions that make someone feel respected—or quietly dismissed. Some of the advice here is blunt, some oddly poetic, and some unmistakably from another era, but the message underneath is familiar. Most marital damage isn't caused by dramatic blowups. It comes from careless remarks, public jokes that land wrong, and moments where being "right" overtakes being kind. In short, this chapter is a reminder that how you actually treat your wife day-to-day matters far more than how you *intend* to treat her. And that you shouldn't go to bed angry at each other.

Don't tell your wife the good story that Smith gave you if you wouldn't have told it [to] her before you were married. By so doing, you lower yourself in her eyes and further show that your respect for her is not what it used to be. Don't fall into the error of thinking that because "it's only husband and wife," it doesn't matter. ✓

Do not neglect to give credit occasionally where it is due.

Think over your wife's job sometimes and ask yourself how you would like to do it.

Don't force your own opinion on your wife—even if you know that it's right—to the extent of being cruel. If she is certain there is a burglar downstairs, get up and look round, and reassure her on the point—otherwise she may lie awake the greater part of the night in a state of terror. →

Do refrain from treating your wife as a plaything, endeavouring to wrap her in cotton wool, or sheltering her from every wind that blows. After all, she is your copartner, and as such, you should allow her to shoulder a certain amount of responsibility. →

Do take care not to make fun of your wife's little foibles in front of other people. She may join in the joke and laugh at them herself, but you are asking for a bad ten minutes when your visitors have gone. ♦

Do make a point of remembering all anniversaries. To forget your wife's birthday or the wedding anniversary is, in her eyes, a crime little short of treason and one which you will have the greatest trouble in explaining.

Do not neglect to give that kiss on leaving in the morning or on returning at night, and don't let it develop into a mere peck. ♦ Take care too that it doesn't become part of a mere routine but retains its warmth.

Do make a note of the fact that a little present unexpected is much more delightful to a wife than a big one long expected. ✓

Don't allow your wife to have to repeat a request that is reasonable. To use the old army phrase, "Jump to it."

Do learn the lesson of bearing and forbearing quite early in your married life. Remember those lines of Cowper:

The kindest and the happiest pair

Will find occasion to forbear;
And something, every day they live.
To pity, and perhaps forgive.

Don't trouble your wife to do something which you can just as easily do for yourself. She is your co-partner, not your servant.

Don't become thoughtless regarding your immediate circle, and especially as regards your wife. Take to heart the words of Sir Humphrey Davy: "Life is made up, not of great sacrifices or duties, but of little things, in which smiles and kindnesses and small obligations, given habitually, are what win and preserve the heart, and secure comfort."

Do at times recall the happy hours of your early love when you were only too happy to have the privilege of fetching and carrying. Still make it your duty and pleasure to open the door, carry the heavy parcel, place the chair at the table, and generally give the right of way to your wife.

Don't reserve your best manners for special occasions and persons outside the family. Remember that your wife has always the first claim on them.

Don't forget that the only way to domestic happiness is the cultivation by both parties of absolute unselfishness.

Don't allow yourself to be angry at the same time as your wife, or certainly the rift will be made worse. Further, don't shout at her unless the house is on fire. ◆

Do take occasion at times to tell your wife that you still love her. Because she is a woman, she likes to hear it and to be assured of it.

Do realise that a little persuasion will attain far better results than a lot of compulsion. A woman is like tar, only melt her, and she will take any form in which you like to mould her. ✦

Don't ever taunt your wife with a past mistake. Let the dead past bury its dead.

Don't forget that a man shows himself a true gentleman, and to his best advantage, when he takes a pleasure in waiting on his wife and carrying out gladly little services for her.

Do try, if in any way angry with each other, to follow out the old Scriptural injunction not to let the sun go down upon your wrath.

Don't talk at your wife either alone or in company, and don't be guilty of the meanness of making remarks at her expense. Don't forget that she belongs to you, and to decry your own is the worst kind of foolishness.

Don't visit upon your wife the ill humor caused by snubs or rebuffs that you have received during the day. This is only a cowardly form of retaliation. Remember that a woman possesses more delicate organisms and is made of finer clay than man. ⊕ It is a well-known law of the animal kingdom that the male of the species always roars when he is irritated, but there is no need for you to bring yourself down to the level of the beast.

Do remember, there can only be true happiness where there is self-denial. The ideal union is where each strives to yield to the reasonable wishes of the other.

NOTES FROM THE HUSBAND SCHOOL:

✓ Timeless Advice
"…because 'it's only husband and wife,' it doesn't matter."

This is a quiet but important reminder. Familiarity doesn't lower the standard of respect; it raises it. The person closest to you deserves your best behavior, not what's left over.

➜ Ahead of Its Time
"…if she is certain there is a burglar downstairs, get up and look round…"

This is emotional intelligence before anyone called it that. Arguing about probabilities won't help someone who's scared at 2 a.m. Getting out of bed and checking does, even if you're certain there's no burglar, and you'd prefer to stay under the warm blankets. The sacrifice costs little and means a lot.

➜ Ahead of Its Time
"…she is your copartner… allow her to shoulder a certain amount of responsibility."

For its era, this is a notably grown-up take. The author frames marriage as a shared responsibility rather than as a matter of protection or control, a view far from universal at the time. Calling your wife a "copartner" signals trust and a recognition that adulthood runs in both directions.

◆ Hidden Gem
"…you are asking for a bad ten minutes when your visitors have gone."

This line understands social reality perfectly. If you embarrass your wife in front of others, you haven't "gotten away with it"—you've merely booked yourself a private follow-up meeting. And it's not going to be a pleasant one.

◆ Hidden Gem
"Don't let [the kiss] develop into a mere peck."

Small rituals carry more weight than they appear to. A kiss that's warm and present reinforces connection in a way no grand gesture can replace. When affection becomes automatic, it also becomes forgettable. One must keep those home fires burning.

✓ Timeless Advice
"A little present unexpected is much more delightful… than a big one long expected."

This is one of marriage's best return-on-investment strategies. A small, unexpected gesture lands far better than a grand one that's been advertised for weeks. (In *The New Husband's Survival Guide*, we tout the power of "Just Because Flowers," which provide oversized bang for the buck.)

◆ Hidden Gem
"Don't shout at her unless the house is on fire."

This is excellent advice disguised as a punchline. If the house is not on fire, shouting is probably not helping. And if the house is on fire, you have bigger problems than winning the argument.

⊕ Vintage POV
"A woman is like tar, only melt her, and she will take any form…"

This metaphor is very much of its time, and best read as such. The author is reaching for an image of persuasion rather than force, but the language reflects a world in which women were far too often discussed as material to be shaped. The underlying idea still holds: gentle influence works better than compulsion.

⊕ Vintage POV
"…a woman possesses more delicate organisms and is made of finer clay…"

This passage attempts to compliment women but ultimately reveals the worldview of its moment. "Finer clay" sounds poetic, but it also portrays women as more fragile, a perspective that hasn't aged as well as the rest of the advice. Read this as cultural context, not modern biology.

III
Conversation

THE HUSBAND SCHOOL OVERVIEW:

Here we address what actually comes out of your mouth—and how often it should have stayed there. It tackles the everyday mechanics of talking and listening, especially the kind that happens at home, when you're tired, distracted, or convinced you're right. Some of the advice here feels timeless, some a little prim, and some unexpectedly sharp about how words land when they're careless, repetitive, or aimed more at winning than understanding. What comes through clearly is that—whether in the 1930s or today—good conversation isn't about being clever or dominant. It's about tact, restraint, and remembering that the people closest to you hear you the most.

Do take every care to make yourself a good conversationalist both at home and abroad. To be able to talk fluently and concisely has carried many men into good positions to which their abilities alone would never have entitled them. ◆

Don't fall into the vulgar and common error of talking for the sake of talking. ◆ Try to achieve brevity in your conversation. Express your thoughts in as few words as possible, and if you want to carry conviction, don't repeat yourself. In the case of most people, their conversation would best begin where they mean to leave off.

Don't consider that conversation is something which you should monopolise. Give other people a chance. Some people's idea of conversation is a never-ending monologue.

Don't be so anxious to come in with something smart that you pay no attention to what is being said. The result will probably be that your comment, when uttered, will be quite irrelevant.

Do be careful not to criticise the imperfections of other people, even if they are apparently strangers to the company you are in at the moment. You can never be certain in this world of who's who.

Don't boast of the success of your children or your relatives. It's only a form of boosting yourself.

Don't let your conversation be of the type that has been described as honey abroad and vinegar at home. ✓ Preserve your nicest sentiments for those who belong to you.

Do be careful to be kind in your talk of others. Follow the example of Joubert, who wrote: "When my friends are blind of one eye, I look at them in profile." ♦

Don't break in when someone else is speaking. A good listener is always appreciated. Learn to take your share of listening as well as talking.

Don't be a person with a grievance if you wish to be popular. The world hasn't much time for the person who harps on one string.

Don't let all your remarks savour of criticism. A little of this sort of thing is perhaps bracing, but too much of it will cause depression.

Don't forget that if you have to tell a home truth, it

should only be necessary to tell it once and not to re-tell it. Further, if it is not a pleasant one, try to tell it with tact and sympathy. Don't, unless in the very exceptional case, rub it in.

Do remember that loud argument is one of the most common signs of faulty education and ill-breeding.

Don't pride yourself on the fact that you always speak as you feel. It is more than probable that you do nothing of the kind, and if you do, it won't be long before you upset someone. An ounce of tact will usually carry you much farther than a ton of such speaking.

Do endeavour to keep your temper even when your views are opposed by those with whom you are conversing. You may of course be right—but so may they.

Don't allow yourself, when engaged in conversation, to be self-conscious or shy. If you fix your mind on what you are going to say, your nervousness will disappear.

Do be careful how you discuss mutual friends with someone else. Words often become strangely twisted in the course of transit and sometimes bear no resemblance to their original signification.

Don't discuss personal affairs in general conversation, and try to steer clear of the personal affairs of other people. Matters that may be of great interest to you are not necessarily so to others.

Don't attempt to help out the man who is somewhat slow of expression by finishing his sentences for him. It implies that in this matter, you consider yourself very much his superior.

Don't allow yourself to become careless in your conversation and, as far as possible, don't use the cant expressions of the moment. Try to avoid describing a thing as "awfully nice" or "putrid."

Notes from The Husband School:

⊕ Vintage POV
Conversation as a path to advancement

In this era, good conversation wasn't just pleasant; it was career equipment. Talking fluently could smooth over a surprising number of shortcomings. A reminder that polish has long been mistaken for competence. For good or for bad, that holds true today.

◆ Hidden Gem
"Don't fall into the vulgar ... error of talking for the sake of talking."

This line understands that not every pause needs rescuing. Talking just to hear yourself speak usually adds noise, not value. Sometimes the smartest contribution is stopping a sentence early. "Wise men speak because they have something to say; Fools speak because they have to say something" – Plato

✓ Timeless Advice
"Don't let your conversation be ... honey abroad and vinegar at home."

This line nails a common blind spot. Too many people save their patience and charm for strangers, leaving the leftovers for home. If anyone deserves your best, kindest conversational self, it's the person who lives with you.

◆ Hidden Gem

"When my friends are blind of one eye, I look at them in profile."

This is a graceful way of describing selective kindness. Everyone has flaws, and friendship works better when we don't insist on staring them in the face. Turning slightly away can be an act of generosity.

⚤ Vintage POV
"Loud argument is… a sign of faulty education and ill-breeding."

The language here reflects strong class assumptions of the time. Calm speech was equated with refinement, while loud disagreement was treated as a social failing. The advice tells us as much about hierarchy as it does about conversation.

➜ Ahead of Its Time
"An ounce of tact will usually carry you much farther than a ton of such speaking."

This is a surprisingly modern insight for its time. Blurting out "how you really feel" may seem brave, but it rarely gets you where you want to go. Tact isn't dishonesty; it's strategy.

ⓘ Modern Translation
"Awfully nice" / "putrid"

These were catch-all expressions of the time, used when someone had run out of precise language. The author's point still holds: vague, overused phrases drain meaning from conversation. When everything is "awfully nice" or "putrid," nothing really is. Precision beats fashionable filler in any decade.

IV
Personal Habits

THE HUSBAND SCHOOL OVERVIEW:

This chapter lives in the small moments: how you leave a room, how you take up space, and how much attention you pay to the people sharing it with you. It's about the actions that seem too minor to matter, until they happen every day. Some of the advice here is practical, some oddly specific, and some quite insightful about how irritation builds—until it turns into a bigger, awkward conversation you didn't see coming. What it all highlights is the same truth: daily behavior is where consideration shows up (or doesn't). And a sunny disposition goes a long way toward making a household a brighter place.

Don't squeeze the tube of tooth paste from the top instead of from the bottom. This is one of the small things of life that always irritates a careful wife. ◆

Do remember to shake out your pipe and put down your book a little earlier than usual if your wife has had a troublesome day with baby and is likely to have to get up and attend to him once or twice during the night.

Do, if you wish for happiness, refrain from adopting the attitude of "that's my way and so you must put up with it."

Your wife may allow you to drop cigarette ash all over the house, or leave everything just where you have finished with it, but it won't make her any better pleased with you.

Don't confine your acts of courtesy to your wife's pretty girl friends. Be as ready to see Miss Prudence Dowdy, who is very much of a bore, back to her home as you would the charming Miss Dolly Dimple. ⓘ

Don't think that your wife has placed waste-paper baskets in the rooms as ornaments. They are put there for you to use. Don't, however, utilise them for spent matches unless you are very well insured.

Don't—if you have no business that takes you abroad—be always about the house. Have a fixed period during which you go out or go away into your den. → Remember that even if you have no calls on your time, your wife has her daily round of duties to get through and, pleasurable as your company may be, there is always the possibility of having too much of a good thing. It is surprising how many wives who love their husbands look forward with dread to the day of their retirement from business. ◆

Do cultivate the habit of believing in yourself if you wish others to believe in you. Let your outlook on life be hopeful, cheery, and optimistic.

Don't get into the habit of storing up a lot of useless old stuff and then grumble for a week if your wife disposes of some of it. Every woman likes her house to be a home, not a marine store depot. Have an occasional overhaul of your belongings and clear out what is useless. You won't require three old hats and four old suits for gardenwear.

Don't be one of those persons who try to run their own life and that of everyone around them according to programme. They usually only succeed in making everyone miserable. Bring a little give-and-take into life.

Do remember that if you are going to get the best out of life, you must overlook a great many things. Your standard is not that of everyone, nor will they see with your eyes. Try sometimes to look at matters from the point of view of the other person.

Do try not to waste time and energy on the non-essentials of life, but to concentrate on the essentials. Don't be one of those persons who flies into a passion and upsets the whole house because someone has taken a book from one shelf of the bookcase and put it back on another. The energy you have spent in railing against this little slip would probably be sufficient to do that pressing job in the garden that you have neglected so long.

Do be careful in your choice of friends. Instinctively, we absorb from them their qualities, and if these are not good, there will inevitably be a decline in our character.

Do cultivate the habit of coming down to breakfast with a smile. Remember that, as the head of the house, it is your duty to see that everyone starts the day in an atmosphere of happiness. ⚚

Don't refrain from singing in your bath if you feel like it. Your wife will welcome it since it's a sign that the barometer is at "set fair."

Do try not only to give out sunshine to others but to imbibe it. Cultivate by every means in your power the sunny side of your nature. Learn to join in the joy of others and to make it your own. Don't reply simply "Yes" when your little daughter asks if you don't think her new doll is lovely. Spread yourself a little in your reply. Share her enthusiasm, and you will double her joy. ➜

Do be not only courteous but properly courteous. If you don't want to be mistaken for a groom, don't raise your hat by touching the brim. Raise it clear of the head for a moment.

Don't expect to be numbered among the good-mannered if you use a nail file, comb, or toothpick otherwise than in a dressing-room.

Don't omit, if seated, to rise when introduced either to a lady or a gentleman. Life is not so short that it does not provide time enough for courtesy.

Don't forget that courtesy is always in fashion and always good form. The small courtesies sweeten life, the greater ennoble it.

Do remember that kindness is a passport which will take you anywhere in the world. It is the golden chain by which society is bound together.

Do try to leave your room as neat as you can. If you don't, you can't grumble if your things are not put back in the place where you expect to find them. You may be untidy in your office—though this is not advisable—but home is a different matter.

Don't be so anxious to get on in the world that you've no time for anything else. Success will probably turn to ashes if by the time you find you have attained your desire, you realise that you are almost a stranger to your wife and children. To work hard for your wife and family is quite laudable, but in doing so, preserve a well-balanced mind and give them their fair share of your time and your attention.

Don't be one of those persons who blame but never praise. If your wife makes some little dish of which you are very fond, don't omit to show your appreciation. If she looks particularly nice on some occasion, don't hesitate to tell her so. A little attention to such things makes the wheels of life run much more smoothly.

Notes from The Husband School:

◆ Hidden Gem
"Don't squeeze the tube of tooth paste from the top…"

This is one of the most domestic arguments in human history. The author understands that tiny habits can carry outsized emotional weight. Toothpaste isn't really the issue; it's the feeling that someone isn't paying attention. Small irritations add up faster than we like to admit.

ⓘ Modern Translation
"Miss Prudence Dowdy" and "Miss Dolly Dimple"

These names are fictional shorthand, not real people. "Prudence Dowdy" represents the dull guest; "Dolly Dimple" the charming one. The message: Courtesy isn't selective. Politeness counts most when it's extended to people who don't entertain you.

➜ Ahead of Its Time
"Have a fixed period during which you go out or go away into your den."

Long before "man caves" and noise-canceling headphones, this author understood the value of personal space. Absence, in reasonable doses, really does make affection grow fonder. Loving someone doesn't mean hovering near them at all times. Sometimes the kindest move is getting out of the way.

Personal Habits

◆ Hidden Gem
"...wives who love their husbands look forward with dread to the day of their retirement from business."

This observation is quietly poignant, and still relevant today. Retirement changes routines, space, and expectations all at once. Love doesn't automatically solve those adjustments. Retirement works best when it's a transition, not a sudden relationship makeover.

⌗ Vintage POV
"As the head of the house... come down to breakfast with a smile."

The hierarchy here is unmistakable. Still, the underlying idea is familiar: Moods are contagious. Starting the day with warmth sets a tone that others feel. Leadership, in this context, is emotional rather than authoritative.

➜ Ahead of Its Time
"Share her enthusiasm, and you will double her joy."

This is the original "girl dad" advice, decades before the phrase existed. Matching a child's enthusiasm costs almost nothing and pays off immediately. You're not praising the doll; you're validating the feeling. Few things make a bigger impression.

⌗ Vintage POV
"Don't... if you use a nail file, comb, or toothpick otherwise than in a dressing-room."

This is pure period etiquette. Grooming rituals were tightly regulated, and public personal maintenance was frowned upon. The advice tells us more about social expectations than hygiene. Consider it a snapshot of how seriously manners were once taken—a time when even a toothpick had to know its place.

✓ Timeless Advice
"Don't be so anxious to get on… that you are almost a stranger to your wife and children."

This warning lands just as hard now as it did then. Providing for your family matters, but being present matters, too. Success feels hollow when the people you worked for barely know you. Balance isn't optional; it's the whole point.

V
Dress and Clothing

The Husband School Overview:

The focus isn't really about cuffs, collars, or whether anyone should ever wear a white waistcoat with a dinner jacket. It's about effort and what your appearance quietly says to the person standing next to you. The advice ranges from impressively specific to surprisingly sharp about pride, comfort, and the slow creep of "good enough." Beneath the period fashion rules is a simple idea that still lands: how you show up matters, especially at home. Dressing well isn't about vanity or impressing strangers. It's a visible way of saying, "I still care." In marriage, that message never goes out of style—even if those loud "plus fours" mercifully did.

Don't make the common mistake of thinking that indifference to dress denotes either individuality or humility. In most cases, it is simply a form of silly pride. Moreover, don't forget that neglect of it is not much of a compliment to either your wife or family. Bear in mind the old couplet:

> *Virtue may flourish in an old cravat*
> *But men and Nature scorn the shocking hat.*

Do be careful in your general turn-out. To be badly groomed or improperly dressed carries with it a certain sense of inferiority and, therefore, loss of power. You can never hope to succeed to the full where there is such loss of energy and of self-confidence.

Don't allow yourself to become careless in the matter of dress in the home, nor permit your wife to be so. To sit down to dinner in the hot weather in your shirt-sleeves may be very comfortable, but no nice woman looks with equanimity on any action that her husband would hesitate to do in the presence of other women.

Don't fall into the error of thinking that the possession of much jewellery marks you as a person of consequence. The wearing of this by men has now gone out of fashion, and where precious stones are worn, they should be of the smallest. At the most, one good ring is the limit allowed by good taste.

Don't endeavour to persuade your wife to refuse invitations because the acceptance will mean that you have to put on your dress-clothes. This is pure selfishness on your part, so for once put your own inclinations on one side and give her a chance of wearing her pretty frocks.

Do be careful not to wear a made-up tie with evening wear or coloured socks with evening shoes. The latter should be plain black silk. Don't forget that if you are in doubt as regards the wearing of tails or a dinner jacket, the former is always in better taste, except in the case of an informal dinner.

Do be careful when selecting a striped tie not to purchase the colours of some famous school or club. It is somewhat awkward to be taken for a Guards officer when the nearest claim you can make to belonging to the Services is that you were once a Boy Scout.

Don't neglect your wife's advice on matters pertaining to your own dress. As a rule, a woman knows better than a man what suits him, and in any case, she knows what she prefers. ✔

Don't grumble when your wife raises the question of a new hat and go on to point out that your present one has lasted you two years. The wearing by a woman of a hat and other things, even only six months behind the fashion, announces to all her friends that she is the unfortunate possessor of a stingy husband. ✦

Do make every endeavour that your dress shall be neat, quiet, and suitable for the occasion. These are the three essential qualities for a well-dressed man.

Don't forget also that a man is well-dressed when you don't know what he is wearing. To dress in a conspicuous manner usually means that the person guilty of it has run off the rails of good taste. ◆

Don't omit to make a note of the fact that soft shirts should never be worn with full dress.

Don't wear a white waistcoat with a dinner-jacket. The experiment has been tried, but it soon died a natural death.

Do take care that you never wear a blazer with anything but white flannels, even if the crest on it is gorgeous enough to stagger humanity.

Do remember that the use of a comb in public is always offensive and against the canons of good taste.

Do, when going out with your wife, dress with the same care that you used to do before you were married. Even if a woman has been married twenty years, she still takes pride in seeing her man well turned out. ✔

Don't turn up to tea in your old gardencoat when your wife has some particular friends coming. It won't take a minute or two to run upstairs and change it, and your wife will think a lot more of you for this deference to her wishes. Remember that it is often the little sacrifices that appeal to women more than the bigger ones. ♦

Don't stick to a style of dress that your wife doesn't like. You may think you look very "nutty" in your somewhat loud plus fours, but if she says they don't suit you, she is probably right.

Don't expect your wife to make a dress last as long as your mother does. The dear old lady has probably now reached the age when she only wishes to be clothed, whereas your wife is still young enough to be dressed.

Do try not to be conservative in the matter of your wife's dresses. Because you liked the blue dress that she wore when you first met her, don't suggest that she should always adopt that colour. Dress is about the one thing in which a woman likes to be adventurous, so let her have her way even if you don't agree with the result.

Don't forget that little adjuncts to dress are always acceptable to a woman. You may not be able to afford a fur coat, but an occasional pair of gloves is always a delight.

Don't be careless and go to the office in that grease-spotted coat. If noticed there, it won't be put down to your credit. A little time and petrol is all that is required.

⚜

NOTES FROM THE HUSBAND SCHOOL:

⊕ Vintage POV
"To sit down to dinner… in your shirt-sleeves…"

The logic is unmistakably old-school: If you wouldn't do it

in front of other women, don't do it at home. The framing hasn't aged well, but the underlying concern—taking pride in how you show up—still resonates. Even if shirt-sleeves (that is, wearing a shirt but no jacket) is practically formal dress today.

✓ Timeless Advice
"Don't neglect your wife's advice on matters pertaining to your own dress."

This is simple, practical wisdom that ages remarkably well. Your wife has a better view of you than you do, literally and figuratively. Ignoring her input has a way of making you look bad—again, literally and figuratively.

⊕ Vintage POV
"...announces to all her friends that she is the unfortunate possessor of a stingy husband."

This line captures the social pressure of the time perfectly. A woman's appearance was often read as a public referendum on her standing—and her husband's generosity. Fashion wasn't just personal style; it was silent messaging. Read this as a snapshot of how status once traveled through hats.

◆ Hidden Gem
"A man is well-dressed when you don't know what he is wearing."

Good style draws attention to the person, not the outfit. If people remember the jacket more than the man, something went wrong. True style is forgettable in the best possible way.

✓ Timeless Advice
"Dress with the same care that you used to do before you were married."

This is a reminder that effort shouldn't stop once commitment starts. Dressing well signals respect, not vanity. It says, "You still matter to me." That message never goes out of fashion.

◆ Hidden Gem
"Little sacrifices… appeal to women more than the bigger ones."

This is the long game of marriage in one sentence. Big gestures are memorable, but regular acts of consideration are felt. They show up daily, which is where relationships actually live. Few insights here are more practical.

ⓘ Modern Translation
"You may think you look very 'nutty' in your somewhat loud plus fours …"

"Nutty" meant eccentric or flashy, and "plus fours" were the colorful, baggy pants of their day. The warning is really about loud personal style: Just because it stands out doesn't mean it works. And if your wife says it doesn't suit you, trust her. She's got the better angle.

VI
FINANCE

THE HUSBAND SCHOOL OVERVIEW:

This chapter addresses money. Not as math, but as manners. It's about what happens when finances quietly turn into leverage, resentment, or a running tally of who "deserves" what. Some of the advice here feels remarkably modern, some unmistakably pre-credit-card, and some blunt enough to end an argument before it starts. What emerges is that marriage shouldn't be one person calling the shots while the other files the receipts. Pride, secrecy, and keeping up appearances do more damage than a sloppy budget ever could. The takeaway is clear: money works best in a marriage when it's handled with transparency, restraint, and a shared sense that you're on the same team.

Don't think that because you earn the money, you are entitled to spend the bulk of it on yourself. Remember that you are partners in a joint concern and that your wife has as much right to her proper share as you have to yours. Don't let the one-time promise "with all my worldly goods I thee endow" be entirely forgotten. ➜

Do try, as far as lies in your power, to give your wife a set sum for housekeeping and another for her own personal use.

It is very lowering to her dignity to have to ask you for money every time she wants to buy a pair of gloves or make a small present to anyone. Give her as good an allowance as you can for dress and pocket money, and impress upon her the necessity of keeping within it. ➔

Don't be so absorbed in making a living that you have no time to make a life. ✓

Do take care not to be led into expenses that you cannot afford in order to keep up appearances. The attempt to do this is only too often accompanied by vulgarity and disastrous consequences. ✓

Don't be led into the error of buying things simply because they are cheap. If you don't really want them, they are dear at any price.

Don't grudge spending money on labor-saving devices. It should be your endeavor to do anything you can to lighten your wife's daily round.

Do avoid the somewhat common practice of having a joint banking account on which you can both draw. Let your wife have a separate account, and you will then both know just how you stand. ➔

Don't let economising be something which the wife alone has to do. See what you can do as regards [to] cutting down your own personal expenses. Watch your expenditure on tobacco, drinks, and amusements.

Don't cut down the household allowance and then grumble because things are not as they were. You can't eat your cake and have it, and your wife can't increase the value of a pound to thirty shillings.

Don't let all your energies be spent upon mere money making. There are other things that matter, such as beauty and love, and it should be your endeavour to put these into your life. ◆

FINANCE

Do try as far as possible to avoid letting accounts run. It's probably not so easy to pay in a month's time as it is to-day. Endeavour to settle on a weekly basis and see that your wife does the same. ⓘ

Don't forget that the quality that will do you most harm financially is pride. ♦ Probably the largest proportion of bankruptcies come from those who have gone beyond their means in pretending that they are what they really are not.

Don't do all the ordering because you think that your wife is wanting in the money sense. This lowers both her dignity and her position. Take a little trouble to teach her, and let her realise that she must cut her coat according to her cloth.

Do take care not to hand out the household allowance as if you were parting with money for which you get little value. If you are not satisfied, go through the bills with your wife and thrash the matter out thoroughly.

Don't run your finances on a haphazard principle. Take your weekly income and split it up into rent and rates, household expenditure, wife's allowance, savings, and extras, and then stick to such allotments. If you adhere rigidly to this, you will never have those unexpected bills that you cannot meet.

Don't forget that life is full of the unexpected. Make provision for such things as doctor's bills, replacements, and breakages. (See extras in preceding paragraph.)

Do make a start, directly you get married, to insure your life. Whatever happens, your wife will then have something to fall back upon.

Notes from The Husband School:

→ **Ahead of Its Time**
"Don't think that because you earn the money, you are entitled to spend the bulk of it on yourself…"

This is a strikingly modern idea for its time. The author flatly rejects the idea that a paycheck equals exclusive spending authority. Instead, marriage is treated like a joint venture, not a solo act with a dependent. Plenty of modern arguments could end right here.

→ **Ahead of Its Time**
"Give your wife a set sum for housekeeping and another for her own personal use… it is very lowering to her dignity to have to ask…"

This isn't really about budgeting; it's about dignity. Having to ask for money puts one adult in a permanently subordinate position. The author recognizes that autonomy matters, even in small purchases. That insight feels quietly progressive.

✓ **Timeless Advice**
"Don't be so absorbed in making a living that you have no time to make a life."

This sentence has aged like a proverb. You can win at work and still lose at home if you're not careful. Money keeps the lights on, but it doesn't raise kids or sustain relationships. A good living shouldn't erase the life it was meant to support.

✓ **Timeless Advice**

"Do take care not to be led into expenses that you cannot afford in order to keep up appearances."

This warning pairs well with the earlier insight on pride. Spending to impress others usually backfires. Appearances are expensive, and the bill eventually comes due. Living within your means is still underrated wisdom.

→ Ahead of Its Time
"Avoid the practice of having a joint banking account... let your wife have a separate account."

This advice runs against what many people assume is "traditional." Separate accounts are framed here as clarity and respect, not secrecy. The author understood that financial independence can actually reduce conflict.

◆ Hidden Gem
"There are other things that matter, such as beauty and love."

This line gently widens the frame beyond money. Financial success isn't the same as a successful life. Beauty, love, and meaning don't show up on balance sheets, but they're what make the numbers worthwhile.

ⓘ Modern Translation
"Avoid letting accounts run... endeavour to settle on a weekly basis."

In a pre-credit economy, unpaid bills were a constant risk. Paying weekly wasn't obsessive; it was basic financial sense. Today, the mechanics have changed, but the warning hasn't: The longer you ignore paying your bills, the louder they eventually get.

◆ Hidden Gem
"The quality that will do you most harm financially is pride."

This is a quiet but shrewd insight. Financial trouble often starts with image management, not necessity. Pride nudges people to spend money they don't have to look like someone they're not. That trap of "keeping up appearances" hasn't gone anywhere.

VII
Health

THE HUSBAND SCHOOL OVERVIEW:

Here is a reminder that your health doesn't exist in a vacuum. It lives in your house with other people. It's not about heroic fitness regimes; it's more about what happens when you're tired, run-down, or ignoring obvious warning signs—and everyone else has to deal with the fallout. The author has strong opinions about sulking at breakfast, powering through headaches, and fresh-air faddists. What comes through, sometimes gently and sometimes not, is that taking care of yourself isn't self-indulgent; it's preventative maintenance for the marriage. If your lifestyle leaves you irritable, exhausted, or snapping at innocent bystanders, something's off. Feeling well, it turns out, is good relationship advice.

Do remember that in the preservation of health, there is no agent so powerful as work. "Work," writes Dean Farmer, "is the best birthright that man still retains. It is the strongest of moral tonics, the most vigorous of mental medicines."

Don't worry yourself into a low condition by mourning over past failures. Turn your back on the shadows and face the light. If there is a fancied skeleton in the cupboard, inter it decently and then flood the place with sunshine. ➜

Do steer clear of any form of recreation which results in your snapping everyone's head off at the breakfast table and which sends you to your work unrefreshed, languid, and in the worst of tempers. ◆

Do realise that if you really are out of sorts, there is no necessity to take it out [on] the family. Your wife has probably enough to do nursing you without having to put up with your ill-temper as well. ✓

Don't allow yourself, as the years go on, to give way and grow slack. Try to preserve that firm step and straight back as long as you possibly can. In the first place, it's a great adjunct to health, and in the second, you don't want to lose the pride which your wife took in these matters.

Do suppress that tendency to fidget, not so much for the sake of your own health as for that of your wife's. We all know the type of man (and woman) who is never quiet for a moment, but whose hands or feet are constantly in motion. Such a condition is certainly not good for your own nerves and is doubly worse for those around you.

Don't sit up late, rise late, and then have to run to the office after half a breakfast. No machinery works well if subjected to intermittent strain and stress.

Don't go on when Nature tells you plainly that it's time to call a halt. The constant headache, the general feeling of lassitude, the need for a stimulant of some kind, and the irritability with every one are Nature's danger signals and, if disregarded, calamity will inevitably follow. ➜

Don't think that you can outrage Nature and then put matters right with a few doses of some patent medicine. Her demands are few in number, moderation in eating and drinking, and sufficient outdoor exercise and sufficient rest, but if you don't give her these, you can certainly look out for trouble.

Do take care not to be one of those persons who are always worrying over their health. If you feel really ill, go and see the doctor, but don't refuse to do so and then continue to worry your wife by vague surmises as to what is the matter with you. It's remarkable how many ailments disappear if you engross yourself in something that deeply interests you.

Do guard yourself against becoming a faddist. Everyone realises the benefit of cold baths for those who can stand them, but to take it when you are far from being well, because it is your custom to take a daily one, is the action of a lunatic. Similarly, if you are somewhat of a fresh air fiend, don't insist on bringing the temperature of the house down to freezing point. ⌽ Although you can stand it, other people perhaps can't, and they have a right to be considered also.

Don't forget that as regards both yourself and your family, prevention is better than cure. Twenty-four hours delay in calling in a doctor is often attended by very serious consequences.

Don't be so foolish as to refuse to wear glasses because you think you look a fright in them, and don't temporise by wearing a monocle when what you require is spectacles. ⓘ

Don't be impatient as regards the illnesses of those around you. Because you have perfect health, there is no reason why you need be unsympathetic.

Do remember that to do certain things at fifty means a much greater strain than to do them at forty. Although you may appear to be in the best of health, take stock of yourself occasionally and, in the course of it, ask yourself if all your habits and pursuits are such as are suitable to your years. If not, have a re-adjustment and drop any that may be injurious.

Notes from The Husband School:

→ Ahead of Its Time
"Don't worry yourself into a low condition by mourning over past failures."

This is surprisingly modern advice disguised in poetic language. Obsessing over old failures doesn't make you wiser; it just makes you tired. The author is basically saying: Bury the skeleton, air out the room, and move on.

◆ Hidden Gem
"Steer clear of any form of recreation which results in your snapping everyone's head off at the breakfast table."

This may be the most polite warning about overindulgence ever written. If your idea of fun turns you into a menace at breakfast, something clearly went wrong the night before. Leisure that requires damage control the next morning isn't fun for anyone.

✓ Timeless Advice
"If you really are out of sorts, there is no necessity to take it out on the family."

This is timeless advice with real household value. Being tired, stressed, or under the weather doesn't entitle you to turn the living room into a complaint desk. Your family didn't cause the mood, and they shouldn't have to absorb it.

➜ Ahead of Its Time
"Nature's danger signals... if disregarded, calamity will inevitably follow."

This passage reads like an early warning about burnout. Constant headaches, irritability, and reliance on stimulants aren't badges of honor; they're signals. Powering through isn't heroic if the system breaks.

⌗ Vintage POV
"Don't insist on bringing the temperature of the house down to freezing point."

This captures the era's health fads perfectly. Cold baths, open windows, and fresh air were treated like moral virtues. The advice pushes back gently: Personal health routines shouldn't make everyone else miserable. Wellness stops being virtuous when it becomes selfish.

ⓘ Modern Translation
"Don't refuse to wear glasses... and don't temporise by wearing a monocle."

This is really about vanity interfering with common sense. Glasses were practical; monocles were performative. Choosing image over function didn't fool anyone then, and it doesn't now. Seeing clearly beats looking clever.

VIII
Children

THE HUSBAND SCHOOL OVERVIEW:

This chapter assumes one important thing right up front: children are always watching. Not just during the big, noble moments—but also when you're tired, irritated, contradicting your wife, or negotiating bedtime like a hostage situation. The advice here is noticeably modern. It focuses on how parents speak to each other, how authority is shared (or quietly undermined), and how everyday fairness leaves a deeper impression than lectures ever could. There's an ample amount of wisdom about patience, knowing when to stand firm—and when to get down on the floor to play with the kids. In short, this chapter reminds you that raising children is an opportunity to pass along your best values. And that children should be both seen *and* heard.

Don't let the children look upon you as a grave and solemn person. Unbend sometimes and have a good romp with them. You may find your joints a little stiff afterwards, but you will be surprised to find how light it makes your heart.

Don't omit to show the children a good example.

Children

Remember, they always copy their elders. To make them considerate, thoughtful, and courteous, let them see you displaying these qualities on all occasions.

Do take the utmost care always to honor your wife in the presence of the children. ✓ If they hear you constantly snapping her up or contradicting her, the inevitable result will be that before long they will lose their respect for her and you.

Don't allow one child to interrupt another who is reading or studying. To ensure peace and comfort in a family, each one must realise that consideration for others is an absolute essential.

Don't find fault unless it is quite certain that a fault has been committed, and then speak reprovingly but, at the same time, lovingly. Never punish on mere suspicion, but if guilt is not proved, give the benefit of the doubt. Children have a very keen sense of justice, and the memory of an unmerited punishment will rankle for years. It was undoubtedly a person with no knowledge of the child mind who first suggested that to give a boy an unearned punishment didn't matter, as he was bound to earn it before long.

Do be careful never to countermand any order which your wife has already given to the children. To do so is only to lower her in their eyes and to give them the impression that they can play off one of you against the other. ➜

Don't be impatient when any of the children are fretful or sick. Your wife has quite enough to put up with without your adding to her troubles, and the probability is that when you have a headache, you are no saint yourself.

Don't allow one member of the family to interrupt another when telling a tale or narrating some experience. Elder children are sometimes given to repressing the younger ones in this respect, and this should be stopped at once.

Do encourage your children to take their part in the table conversation. Never act on that idiotic old saying that children should be seen and not heard. ⊕ At the same time, do not let them over-ride the conversation and repress at once any tendency to shout at one another.

Don't forget that the family table is the last place in the world where there should be any unpleasant remarks made. Nothing is worse for digestion than trouble or worry. Let your dinner table be the happy gathering point for the family. See to it that there is no vulgar chipping or decrying of the talents of one member of the family by the others.

Don't pay heavy school fees and at the same time neglect the home discipline. The one is just as important as the other. Family life has been well described as God's own method of training the young.

Do insist that at all times the boys pay proper respect to their mother and sisters. Don't permit too much teasing of the latter or let the boys think that women run secondary in the scheme of things. ➜ See that they always spring to open the door for their mother. The boy who is brought up to pay proper respect to women will find himself welcome and at ease in any good class of society.

Don't forget in all your dealings with the children that kind words are the music of the world.

Don't make a decision and then alter it because one of the children whines or coaxes. Once they realise that this method may be successful, they will protest in some form or other at everything which they don't like. Decide on the course you mean to take and then stick to it.

Don't allow children to be importunate in their

CHILDREN

demands. If they are, and you give way, they will expect more and more.

Do take the utmost care that each member of the family respects the others' privacy. Neglect of this generally means loss of temper and loss of self-respect. Let each person's room, drawer, or even playbox be inviolate and not to be touched by others without permission.

Do endeavour to be as pleasant at your own table as you would be if you were a guest at that of someone else. Surely you should pay as much respect to your own as you would to others. Besides, don't forget that you largely set the standard for the household.

Don't be a prohibitive father. The parent who tells the children ten times what they must not do, for only once what they may do, should not be surprised if they come to look upon him as somewhat of a spoilsport, if not an ogre. ♦

Do as far as possible try to help, and not hinder, natural influences. The boy with a natural aptitude for making things may at times cause a good deal of muddle in the house, but if you repress him entirely, you may be suppressing the genius of a born engineer. ✓

Don't punish the children when you are busy, tired, hungry, or vexed. Wait until you are in a frame of mind when you can act judicially.

Don't send the children to such an expensive school that you can't afford to let them indulge in the same sports, etc., as their schoolfellows. Children are often terrible snobs and will rub in the fact that one of them cannot do the same as the others. This may probably give rise to an inferiority complex that will last through life. Send them to a school where they can join with others on an equal footing.

Don't spend all your money on the training of the boys and leave the girls with an inferior education. They have just as much right to their fair share, and in these days it is just as necessary. ➜

Don't get the idea that what was good enough for you in your youth should be good enough for your children. Times have moved since then. On the other hand, don't start them where you left off. A little hard struggle at the beginning tends to form character.

Notes from The Husband School:

✓ Timeless Advice
"Do take the utmost care always to honor your wife in the presence of the children."

Children learn respect by watching how it's modeled. If they hear you dismiss or contradict your wife, they absorb that lesson instantly. Honor shown in everyday moments carries more weight than lectures. This rule never goes out of date.

➜ Ahead of Its Time
"Do be careful never to countermand any order which your wife has already given to the children."

This is remarkably sophisticated co-parenting advice for its time. Undermining your spouse doesn't just confuse children; it quietly erodes authority. Kids are experts at spotting daylight between parents and learning to play one against the other. Unity here isn't about control; it's about solidarity.

⚘ Vintage POV

Children

"Never act on that idiotic old saying that children should be seen and not heard."

This line is pushing back against a deeply ingrained social rule of the era. Children were expected to be silent, orderly, and invisible. The author rejects that outright. It's a snapshot of parenting norms beginning to shift.

→ **Ahead of Its Time**
"Don't permit... the boys [to think] that women run secondary in the scheme of things."

Strip away the old-fashioned gestures, and the principle is unmistakable. Boys are taught how to treat women long before they realize it. Respect isn't instinctive; it's learned. It's moral education, not etiquette.

◆ **Hidden Gem**
"Don't be a prohibitive father."

This is a sharp observation wrapped in gentle language. A father who only says "no" quickly becomes the household ogre. This line recognizes that joy earns trust faster than constant restriction. Even rules need breathing room.

✓ **Timeless Advice**
"Do as far as possible try to help, and not hinder, natural influences."

This is gentle wisdom that still holds up. Children don't all learn the same way, and forcing them into neat lanes can stifle development. Encouragement works better than suppression. Curiosity is usually pointing somewhere useful.

→ Ahead of Its Time

"Don't spend all your money on the training of the boys and leave the girls with an inferior education."

This passage lands with surprising clarity. The author flatly rejects the idea that girls deserve less because of tradition. Equal opportunity isn't framed as generosity; it's framed as fairness. That's miles ahead of its time.

IX
Recreations

THE HUSBAND SCHOOL OVERVIEW:

The author addresses how you relax—and who pays the price for it. This chapter takes a hard look at hobbies, evenings out, weekends away, and the subtle difference between recreation and quiet selfishness. The author is less concerned with what you enjoy than how you enjoy it: whether your pastimes bring you closer together, leave one person carrying the load, or turn relaxation into another solo pursuit. There's plenty here about shared interests, one-sided "holidays," and hobbies that mysteriously generate work for everyone else. The message is simple but pointed: leisure should restore the household, not drain it. And that you should probably learn to dance.

Don't laugh when you find going shopping with your wife placed under this heading. It is her recreation, and she will think all the more of you if occasionally you put your own inclinations on one side and join forces with her in something in which she is interested.

Do take care that the car doesn't become the leading feature in your life. See that the possession of it doesn't affect adversely the things in which you formerly took pride, such as your house and garden, or, even more important, that it curtails expenditure in things which are much more necessary.

Don't insist upon your wife being always a passenger. Teach her to drive. A long journey is much more enjoyable to both if you can share the labour. →

Do endeavour as far as possible to take up the same recreations. This will give you a joint interest and make you the greater pals.

Don't laugh at your wife's recreations, although they may seem to you absurd. While you are wondering what pleasure she sees in spending two or three hours at a sewing meeting she, on her part, cannot conceive how you can waste your time at that Masonic meeting or public dinner. Don't forget the old adage, "chacun à son goût" (to each his own taste). ✓

Don't, when once you are married, continue a recreation that is highly dangerous. The wife of a man who finds his hobby in motor racing or mountain climbing must often have some very anxious moments.

Do be careful as you grow older not to drop all athletic pursuits unless you want to see your toes gradually disappearing from view. Most women like their husbands to keep slim and fit even with advancing years. Strive to keep your youthful vigour as long as you can.

Do endeavour that at least one of your hobbies is of the description that can be carried out within the home, but, on the other hand, don't let it engross every minute of your time. Take care also that it is not of the type that demands that you shall not be in any way interrupted and imposes silence on the rest of the household.

Don't take up a hobby which entails your getting the pleasure and other people the work pertaining to it. There are some men who claim that their hobby is gardening, but while they leave their wives to do the actual digging, their part is restricted to sitting in an arm-chair and turning it over in their mind. ◆

Don't, unless for some very good reason, put a veto on any recreation your wife may wish to take up. After all, she must have pretty good judgment since she elected to marry you. You wouldn't be at all pleased if she wanted to put her foot on some recreation of yours which, in your opinion, was particularly desirable. ◆

Do refrain from smiling in a superior manner if your wife wishes to attend lectures or classes. Of course, you don't require any further knowledge, but let her alone if she thinks she does. At any rate, it will give her an interest, and she will be a better companion than the wife who only gets her ideas from feminine tea-party chatter.

Don't forget that a sensible hobby tends to longevity. There may come a time when you have perforce to give up your daily work or business, and if you have no hobby to fill up your time, you'll soon fall into the ranks of the arm-chair and slipper brigade.

Do, in choosing a hobby, select one which possesses the double merit of being out of doors and one in which your wife can join. This will give you health and community of interest.

Don't attempt to choose your wife's books for her if she is fond of reading. You may think that the reading of light literature is a waste of time, but to her it is a much needed relief from the daily round. Remember, you are her husband and not her schoolmaster.

Don't, if your wife is fond of it, omit to learn to dance. If you are unable to join with her in this recreation, half the pleasure will be lost to her. Further, in order not to drag you to something in which you cannot participate, she will often feel compelled to stay at home when she would love to be dancing.

Don't take the type of holiday that gives your wife just the same duties that she has at home. You may like a camping holiday, but first ask yourself if this is going to be a restful one for her and if it is going to give her a respite from the preparation of meals. →

Do occasionally put your own inclinations on one side and go out with your wife in the evening to call on friends. Remember that you are mixing with people all day, but that she is more or less shut up in the house and gets little chance of mixing with others. ⌀

Don't spend every evening at the club and return home hoping to find your wife where Cain found his, that is, in the land of Nod. The probability is that she won't be able to go to sleep until you are safely at home. ⓘ

Don't expect your wife to find all her relaxation in needlework or similar pursuits. She probably has ideas of her own, and it is your duty, and should be your pleasure, to fall in with these as far as possible.

Don't take a furnished house for a holiday and at the same time send the maid away for hers. This may be a good arrangement so far as you are concerned, but its result will be that your wife will have a poor time.

Don't let your annual holiday be of the kind that leaves you more tired than when you started. Attempting to see the maximum in the minimum of time is more than foolish. Also, if cruising, don't cut your sleeping time down to the minimum by staying up late every night. Early to bed and early to rise is just as good a rule for the holiday as for the everyday life.

Don't buy a motor cycle and side-car without first

consulting your wife. You may think it splendid to be able to cover so much more ground than you did on the two cycles, but you may find that she is nervous of your suggested means of locomotion. Further, perhaps she is quite content with the more limited range of the push-cycle and prefers the quiet companionable ride to the swift and less conversational rush through the countryside.

Don't let your wife's cycle become, after marriage, only a means of making a hurried run round the shops while you use yours to go off for long rides with your best chum. Take her with you, and even if it reduces your mileage, the pleasure of her company will more than compensate.

NOTES FROM THE HUSBAND SCHOOL:

→ Ahead of Its Time
"Don't insist upon your wife being always a passenger. Teach her to drive."

This is quietly radical advice for its era. Teaching her to drive isn't just practical; it's a power shift. Sharing the wheel means sharing responsibility, fatigue, and decision-making. Turns out equality makes road trips better, too.

✓ Timeless Advice
"Don't laugh at your wife's recreations, although they may seem to you absurd."

This is basic respect, framed plainly. Mocking what brings someone joy doesn't make you insightful; it makes you smaller. Laughing with someone builds connection; laughing at them drains it fast. Respecting her interests costs nothing and avoids a lot of unnecessary friction.

◆ **Hidden Gem**
"Don't take up a hobby which entails your getting the pleasure and other people the work pertaining to it."

This line exposes the classic "armchair hobbyist." Enjoyment should carry its own weight. Fun that generates chores for others is a bad deal. Real hobbies don't outsource the hard part.

◆ **Hidden Gem**
"Don't... put a veto on any recreation your wife may wish to take up... she elected to marry you."

This is a witty reminder about autonomy. Someone capable of choosing a spouse is probably capable of choosing a hobby. Veto power isn't a marriage benefit. Trust is implied in the contract.

➜ **Ahead of Its Time**
"Don't take the type of holiday that gives your wife just the same duties that she has at home."

This is a modern take on the worst kind of vacation. If your wife is still cooking, cleaning, and organizing—just with better views—congratulations, you've relocated the job. A holiday shouldn't come with the same duties and worse cookware. Rest that only applies to one person isn't relaxation.

⊕ Vintage POV
"Remember that you are mixing with people all day... she is more or less shut up in the house."

This is a clear snapshot of domestic life in the 1930s. Men had built-in social interaction; women often didn't. The advice acknowledges that imbalance, even if it accepts the structure behind it. It's a reminder of how isolated home life could be, and how easily that isolation was overlooked.

ⓘ Modern Translation
"Don't spend every evening at the club... hoping to find your wife where Cain found his, in the land of Nod."

"Land of Nod" is a biblical way of saying "fast asleep." The warning is about absence, not clubs. Coming home late and expecting instant domestic peace ignores the anxiety you may have caused. Absence has consequences.

X
Out and About

THE HUSBAND SCHOOL OVERVIEW:

Here we explore what happens once you leave the house, and how easily good intentions can unravel in public. It covers weekends away, dinner parties, car rides, late arrivals, awkward introductions, and all the small social moments where a husband can accidentally create a memory he'd rather not revisit. The author shows a particular sensitivity to how wives get sidelined in public—left waiting, left guessing, or left alone while someone sneaks off to the bar. There's plenty here about punctuality, planning ahead, when not to "make whoopee," and not treating your wife like an accessory you brought along. The moral of the story: when you go out together, your wife's good time should sit at the top of the evening's agenda.

Don't forget when going to stay with friends to notify the hour of your arrival and whether coming by car or train. In the latter case, they will require to know in order to make arrangements to meet you. Further, once you have announced the hour of your departure, stick to it. You may be pressed to go at a later hour, but if you do agree, there is the possibility that you may throw out the daily routine.

Don't commit the unpardonable sin of introducing your wife with "Meet the wife." →

Do take particular care not to be late when invited to a card party. Remember that until you arrive, the tables cannot be made up and that consequently your late arrival is a slight to every one present.

Don't omit when attending any functions, such as an at-home or tea party, to assist the hostess as far as possible by attending on the ladies present.

Do refrain when playing cards commenting on anyone's playing to another person. Post-mortems are never pleasant, and it's a good rule to let the dead past bury its dead.

Don't when playing cards look scornful if the others have an objection to playing for high stakes or for playing for money at all. They have as much right as you to be considered.

Don't when going for a week-end be so careless in your packing that you find it necessary to borrow from your host. Make for the nearest shop or do without.

Do make every endeavour when staying at a boarding-house to fall in with the general temperament. Don't start to make whoopee among a community of elderly people or suggest cards on a Sunday in a house that is strictly Sabbatarian. Try to fit in with your environment. ⓘ

Don't also discuss the shortcomings of the house with other guests. If you have a complaint to make, let it be to the management, and if it is not sufficiently important for that, then be silent.

Don't omit to allow your wife or any lady to precede you into a car or taxi, but take care to get out first in order to assist her to alight. ⌽

Don't forget also to allow your wife or any lady accompanying you to precede you in getting out of a lift.

Do remember in whatever company you may find yourself not to be stand-offish, critical, cynical, or offensive. Don't associate yourself too closely with any particular clique, whether it is in a boarding-house, tennis club, or dance hall.

Don't forget when motoring to acknowledge all signals given by other motorists and also make your own clear and distinct.

Do be considerate and, if your wife is nervous in a car, drive slowly. Don't laugh at her and then go full speed ahead in the idea that you will break her of this trait. By so acting, you will only increase her nervousness, and you certainly won't increase her love for you. ➜

Don't be the owner of a noisy horn and don't sound it too much. The donkey who brays the loudest is not always the most useful animal.

Don't drive in such a manner as to raise clouds of dust, and don't drive so near the kerb on a wet day as to splash pedestrians. Although they may not possess a car, they are still entitled to some consideration.

Don't make the mistake when invited to a birthday or christening party of taking your present with you. This should always be sent in advance.

Don't forget after you have stayed with friends to send the bread and butter letter as soon as possible after your return home. Endeavour also to make it something better than a mere thank you, and where your friends have made an extra effort to give you a good time, take a little trouble to tell them how much you have appreciated it. ⚘

Do strive to get a character for punctuality in all your social engagements. Make it your endeavour to be always present five minutes before the hour fixed. ✓

Don't omit when any lady leaves or enters the room to stand up and to remain so until the door is closed or she has sat down.

Do remember if you form the sudden idea of spending Whitsuntide or Easter at the seaside to give your wife sufficient warning. It's all very well to give her a nice surprise the day before, but she won't thank you for so doing. You may think that it should only take a minute or two to pack a bag, but there are one hundred and one arrangements about the house to be made which cannot be done at a moment's notice. Moreover, there is always the momentous matter of dress to be decided.

Don't rush your wife off to some holiday resort at a time when it is likely to be crowded without making some arrangement beforehand for your accommodation. Long before you have walked round and found a home, she will be worn out and all her pleasure gone, added to which the accommodation you will obtain in these circumstances will probably be of an inferior description.

Don't take your wife to a dance and then leave her to herself for the greater part of the evening while you spend a good time in the card room or the bar. If you do this, you can hardly wonder if she complains that she wishes she had never come. Don't forget that your first duty is to see that she has a good time, and further that the world is quick to notice where a wife is neglected. ✓

⚜

NOTES FROM THE HUSBAND SCHOOL:

➜ Ahead of Its Time
"Don't commit the unpardonable sin of introducing your wife with 'Meet the wife.'"

This is an early takedown of social shorthand that accidentally insults your spouse. "Meet the wife" makes her sound like an accessory rather than a partner. The author is calling for basic dignity before it was fashionable.

ⓘ Modern Translation
"Don't start to make whoopee... or suggest cards on a Sunday in a house that is strictly Sabbatarian."

"Make whoopee" meant lively partying, and "Sabbatarian" meant strict Sunday observance. The advice boils down to reading the room. Every household has its own rhythms and rules. Fitting in shows respect.

⚓ Vintage POV
"Don't omit to allow your wife... to precede you into a car or taxi... get out first to assist her."

This is old-school manners with very specific stage directions. The moves may feel theatrical now, but the intention is clear: notice your wife and help her. Strip away the choreography and what's left is basic thoughtfulness.

➜ Ahead of Its Time
"If your wife is nervous in a car... don't laugh at her and then go full speed ahead."

This is an early lesson in emotional validation. Mockery doesn't cure anxiety; it intensifies it. The author suggests that fear deserves patience, not correction. Empathy makes for better travel companions.

⊕ Vintage POV
"Don't forget after you have stayed with friends to send the bread and butter letter…"

The "bread and butter letter"—a type of formal thank you note—wasn't optional. It was social currency. Mishandling it reflected poorly on the whole family. A glimpse into how seriously manners once traveled.

✓ Timeless Advice
"Do strive to get a character for punctuality… be always present five minutes before the hour fixed."

This isn't about clocks; it's about courtesy. Showing up late quietly tells people their time was optional. Being early is a small discipline with outsized returns. Still true today, still underrated.

ⓘ Modern Translation
"Do remember if you form the sudden idea of spending Whitsuntide… give your wife sufficient warning."

This is the 1930s version of announcing a weekend getaway on Friday night and wondering why no one's pleased. Whitsuntide (formerly a widely observed church holiday) mattered—and so did the invisible prep behind it. Surprise trips are only fun if someone else isn't stuck scrambling.

✓ Timeless Advice

How to Be a Good Husband

"Don't take your wife to a dance and then leave her to herself... your first duty is to see that she has a good time."

This advice is refreshingly clear about priorities. If you bring your wife somewhere, abandoning her is not an option. Presence is the point of going together. A good night out isn't measured by your fun alone.

XI
Entertaining

THE HUSBAND SCHOOL OVERVIEW:

The focus is on what happens when people come over, and how quickly a pleasant evening can go sideways with just a few poorly chosen words. It tackles dinner parties, introductions, small talk, and the dangerous urge to narrate what's wrong with the food, the help, or your own digestive system. The author shows a keen awareness of how easily public critiques, visible sulking, or an unsolicited "organ recital" can undo a wife's hard work before dessert is served. There's plenty here about tact, timing, and knowing when to smile, nod, and stay quiet. Entertaining, it turns out, is less about impressing guests and more about not embarrassing your partner.

Don't criticise the food at your own table when you are entertaining, and especially refrain from doing it before the servants. To do so will only have the effect of making your wife unhappy, rendering your guests uncomfortable, and probably, repeated with additions, cause a small riot in the kitchen. Wait till your guests have departed, and then consult as to the measures to be taken for improvement in the future. ✓

Don't "tell off" a servant in the presence of your guests. It will make the latter feel uncomfortable and may result in the maid following the now common custom of "downing tools." ⓘ In any case, her service for the rest of the day will probably be marked by a surly or a tearful demeanour.

Do make a point of welcoming your wife's friends just as heartily as if they were your own. You may not like Mrs. B., but while she is under your roof, it is the height of bad manners to even let her have a suspicion of the fact.

Don't forget that if your wife is entertaining lady guests, it is your duty to escort them to the front door.

Do endeavour when introducing two guests to each other to bring up some subject in which they will both be interested. It is hardly sufficient to introduce them, remark on the weather, and then leave them to find a subject for themselves.

Don't entertain your visitors with a full and detailed account of your recent illness, giving them a graphic account of every pain you suffered. They have come to your house to be entertained, not to listen to an organ recital. ♦

Don't attempt to give champagne suppers on a soda-water income. Your true friends won't appreciate your efforts as they will feel they are putting you to expense that you can ill afford, while your false friends will only put it down as "swank." ♦

Do take care that your guests will not clash. Don't invite the elderly, stodgy and pompous, even if it is good for your business, at the same time as the young and frivolous. Much better divide it into two separate functions.

Don't chat on the door step with one departing guest, leaving the others to look after themselves.

Don't unduly press your guests to partake of everything on the table. This one-time custom now only exists among semi-civilised peoples. Don't also, in a spirit of false humility, decry what you have provided and suggest that it is not all that it should be. Do the best that you can reasonably afford and leave it at that.

Don't growl every time your wife proposes to ask a few friends in for the evening. You may think it a bit of a nuisance, but you will spoil her pleasure if you let her see that you think so.

Do be careful not to make the mistake of telling your wife that you will be only too delighted if she will go to the pictures, theatre, etc., but that you don't care for that sort of thing and will stop at home and keep house. Prior to your marriage, you would only have been too happy to have gone anywhere with her, and your refusal now cannot fail to hurt her. For once, put your own wishes on one side and accompany her. ➜

Notes from The Husband School:

✓ Timeless Advice
"Don't criticise the food at your own table…"

There are few faster ways to ruin a dinner party than trashing your own meal out loud. You make your wife feel lousy, your guests feel trapped, and the chicken feels personally attacked. Save the critique for later, when no one is holding a fork mid-bite.

ⓘ Modern Translation
"'Downing tools'…"

"Downing tools" was period language for a servant stopping work in protest—a phrase shaped by the labor tensions of the era. The point here isn't politics; it's timing and tact. Public scolding creates predictable consequences. Handle problems privately or expect them to last all evening.

♦ Hidden Gem
"Don't entertain your visitors with a full account of your recent illness…"

The "organ recital" pun was too funny to pass up. Your guests came for dinner, not a narrated tour of your body parts. If people stop chewing, you've gone too far.

♦ Hidden Gem
"Don't attempt to give champagne suppers on a soda-water income."

This is solid advice about honesty, not hosting. Pretending you can afford more than you can just creates stress for everyone involved. True friends don't want you stretching yourself thin for appearances. Comfort beats spectacle.

➜ Ahead of Its Time
"Do be careful not to make the mistake of telling your wife that you will be only too delighted if she will go to the pictures …"

This is the 1930s version of saying, "Have fun. I'll be here not having fun with you." The author notes how quickly romance deflates when enthusiasm fades. You don't have to love the activity; you just have to love the person going with you. Sometimes the date is the point.

XII

Theatres, Dinners, and Restaurants

The Husband School Overview:

This chapter is about going out and not quietly sabotaging the evening once you do. It covers theatre nights, dinners out, and all the small decisions that determine whether the night feels thoughtful or mildly disappointing in ways that will simmer for days. The author is especially tuned in to timing, effort, and the temptation to wander off (usually toward a bar) at exactly the wrong moment. There's also a sharp understanding of anticipation—why arriving early matters, why dressing up still counts, and why remembering the chocolates beforehand earns disproportionate credit. The main takeaway is simple: a night out isn't just about the show or the meal. It's about making your wife feel chosen the entire time you're there. Secondarily, a bottle of crème de menthe rarely hurts your prospects.

Do try to make a practice when taking your wife to the theatre of booking your seats in advance. This will often prevent you from having to pay more than you intended and will obviate your wife having to wait while you stand in a queue.

Don't forget that you precede a lady to a theatre seat, but on reaching the row in which it is situated, you stand on one side and allow her to go first.

Do bear in mind that most ladies like to get to their theatre seats at least five minutes before the curtain goes up in order that they can look around and see who is present and what they wear. ♦

Don't forget that box of chocolates, and if she prefers a particular kind, which is probably not on sale in the theatre, take care to get them beforehand. ⏀

Don't leave your wife alone during the interval in order to go and get a drink. For once, go without. Of course, if she presses you to go, that is a different matter, but satisfy yourself that her pressure is genuine. You will find that she appreciates your sacrifice. →

Don't consider that you have done all that is necessary when you take your wife out to dinner or to a theatre. Pay her the further compliment of getting into dress clothes for the occasion. Such a compliment is one which will condone many of your other sins of omission. ✓

Do be careful not to be too long in depositing your hat, etc., in the cloak-room if your wife is waiting for you. It is embarrassing for any lady to have to wait long in any such public place as the entrance hall of an hotel or theatre.

Don't forget that if following a waiter to a table, a lady should precede her husband. If, on the other hand, they have to seek a table, he should lead the way.

Don't omit, when taking your wife out to dinner at a restaurant, to mark the occasion by suggesting a bottle of wine. Remember that ladies usually prefer a sweet wine to a dry, and that as regards liqueurs, Crème de menthe is always a favourite.

Notes from The Husband School:

◆ Hidden Gem
"Most ladies like to get to their theatre seats [early] …"

This is a quietly perceptive observation about enjoying a night out. The experience starts before the curtain rises: people-watching, outfits, the whole scene. Rushing in late skips half the fun. The atmosphere is part of the show.

φ Vintage POV
"Don't forget that box of chocolates… get them beforehand."

Yes, theater chocolates are the metaphor, but the real message is timeless: Remember her preferences and don't leave it to chance. Nothing says "I tried" like already having the thing she likes.

➜ Ahead of Its Time
"Don't leave your wife alone during the interval…"

This is an argument for presence over personal preference. Ducking out for a drink while your wife waits alone sends a louder message than you think. The author wisely warns that "Do what you want" doesn't always mean "Do what you want."

✓ Timeless Advice
"Pay her the further compliment of getting into dress clothes…"

This isn't about tuxedos; it's about effort. Dressing up signals that the evening matters and that she does, too. Showing up polished is a form of respect. Romance doesn't survive on sweatpants alone.

XIII
General

THE HUSBAND SCHOOL OVERVIEW:

This final chapter is where the author clears his throat, leans back, and says, "All right, now that we've covered everything from carving meat to not sulking at breakfast, let's talk about the point of it all." It's less about rules and more about demeanor: kindness, humor, compromise, and the way small daily choices quietly add up to a life together. There's a strong case made for laughing more, sighing less, and remembering that marriage works a lot like government: Nothing functions if everyone insists on getting their way. If the earlier chapters offered tactics, this one offers perspective. Think of it as the reminder that being decent, optimistic, and occasionally amused by life is still the best long-term strategy—at home and abroad.

Don't be proud of the fact that you can't carve and that you always leave it to your wife. It is the duty of the head of the house to undertake this task, and by handing it over, you confess that you play only the second fiddle.

Don't forget that marriage, like government, must be a series of compromises. ✓

Do make every effort to show kindness whenever possible. Remember that Wordsworth wrote:

> *That best portion of a good man's life,*
> *His little nameless, unremembered acts of kindness*
>   *and of love.* ◆

Don't leave humour entirely out of your life. Remember that it is the lubricant which oils the machinery of life and makes it run smoothly. ◆

Don't forget that you cannot make your presence felt so long as you are not master of yourself.

Do take care not to get into the habit of sighing over what might have been. Put it out of your mind and make the best of what is. Moreover, it may possibly be that what might have been is not half such a rosy picture as your imagination paints it. What about adopting as your motto "The best is yet to be"?

Don't forget that the home is the one place where a man shows whether or not he is truly courteous. → He may be a delightful companion abroad, his manners to the women he meets in society may be perfect, but if he is not considerate towards his own womenfolk, his good form is only a veneer.

Do remember that if you aspire to the good old name of gentleman, your conduct at all times must be marked by consideration for others. This is shown best not in the big things of life but in the little ones.

Do endeavour to take the rough things of life by the smooth handle.

Do try to cultivate the habit of enjoying things and finding pleasure in the small affairs of life. To be able always to look on the sunny side of life is worth far more than a fortune.

Don't look on life through smoked glasses. Bear in mind the following little verse:

Life's a mirror; if we smile.
Smiles come back to greet us;
If we're frowning all the while
Frowns forever meet us.

Don't cultivate the idea that your daily work is dreary and monotonous. Learn to find happiness in the doing of it, and it will seem tenfold lighter. Do realise that all work is ennobling if we put our best into it.

Don't forget that the world has you always more or less under inspection. In this connection, remember the words of Goethe: "Behaviour is a mirror in which everyone shows his image."

Don't grumble if marriage makes you neglect many of the things that you used to do when you were single. It is better to neglect the whole world than your wife. Moreover, if you have chosen wisely, you are much the gainer since a good wife has aptly been described as a gift bestowed upon man to reconcile him to the loss of Paradise. ✓

Do take care that you don't make your wife pay too high a price for any success you may achieve. When this does arrive, the rewards are in no sense equal since the husband gets the glory and the wife only the reflected glory. →

Don't forget that two of the essentials to a happy married life are mutual affection and esteem. These cannot however exist for long unless there is mutual respect and consideration at all times and under all conditions.

Don't ever use that absurd phrase: "It's everyone for himself in this world." Remember that if this theory were generally practised, we should still be in that now far-off age when men took what they wanted by the simple process of clubbing the other fellow on the head. If we accept the privileges of an organised society, we must be prepared to do our share of giving to the common weal.

Do realise that if you are to get the full value out of life, you must live it with all your faculties all the time. Until you come to the time when your physical faculties begin to fail, you should so live your life that every day is just a little too short for what you purpose to do in it. There is a world of truth in the old saying that it's better to wear out than to rust out.

Notes from The Husband School:

✓ Timeless Advice
"Don't forget that marriage, like government, must be a series of compromises."

This may be the most realistic definition of marriage in the book. If everyone insists on getting their way, nothing works. Compromise isn't romantic, but it's highly functional. And like government, it works best when give-and-take feels like progress, not defeat.

◆ Hidden Gem
Wordsworth on "little nameless, unremembered acts of kindness and of love."

This is a reminder that marriage isn't built on grand

moments. It's built on dozens of tiny ones no one posts about. The quiet favors, the unnoticed patience, the small kindnesses that never get named. That's the foundation. Everything else is decoration.

◆ Hidden Gem
"Don't leave humour entirely out of your life."

Humor is treated here not as entertainment, but as maintenance. It reduces friction and maintains perspective. A life without laughter gets heavy fast. A shared sense of humor reminds you why you chose each other in the first place.

➜ Ahead of Its Time
"Don't forget that the home is the one place where a man shows whether or not he is truly courteous."

This is an advanced idea for its time: Character isn't proved in public, it's revealed at home. Anyone can be charming in company. The harder test is how you treat the people who see you every day. Courtesy that disappears at the front door is just a mirage.

✓ Timeless Advice
"It is better to neglect the whole world than your wife."

This is blunt, unapologetic advice about priorities. Marriage doesn't fit neatly around everything else. It comes first, or it slowly erodes. You can disappoint many people and recover. Overlooking your spouse is harder to undo.

➜ Ahead of Its Time

"Don't make your wife pay too high a price for any success you may achieve."

This passage recognizes a truth many couples still wrestle with. Success often has hidden costs, and too often they're paid by someone else. If one partner gets the applause while the other absorbs the strain, something's off.

Closing Thoughts from The Husband School

What This Book Was Really About

If you've made it this far, you've probably noticed the thread running throughout this book. For all the talk of manners, timing, propriety, and self-control, it keeps circling the same quiet truth: marriage isn't tested in dramatic moments. It's tested at home, in small, ordinary ones.

Again and again, the author returns to daily behavior: how you speak when you're tired, how you react when you're irritated, and how much care you take when it would be easier not to. He's far less interested in charm than in character. Less concerned with winning arguments than with not giving them cause to start in the first place.

Strip away the etiquette of the times, and the message is consistent: kindness counts most where it's least visible. Courtesy that disappears at the front door is just performance. And consideration ages far better than authority, cleverness, or being technically right.

In that sense, this book was never really about rules. It was about integrity. How you show up. And how often you choose restraint, humor, and generosity over ego—especially when you'd rather be at the bar than at the theater.

THE PARTS THAT FELT SURPRISINGLY MODERN

One of the unexpected pleasures of reading this book is how often it feels ahead of its time.

The author understood how easily one partner's "relaxation" can become another partner's work. Long before "being present" became a phrase, he warned against husbands who were physically home but mentally elsewhere. He recognized that undermining your spouse—especially in front of the kids—can cause lasting damage.

He even grasped something many modern books still struggle to say plainly: fairness isn't just about how things turn out in the end; it's about how they feel while they're happening. Being left waiting. Being left guessing. Being left stranded in public while someone else enjoys themselves in the card room.

None of this is delivered with modern language. There are no frameworks, acronyms, or five-step systems. But the instincts are there: partnership over performance, awareness over entitlement, and a steady reminder that marriage works best when both people feel considered.

It's striking how often the advice sounds less like a relic and more like something you'd hear today, minus the podcast theme music.

THE PARTS THAT AGED—AND WHY THAT'S FINE

Of course, not everything here travels gracefully across nine decades.

There are hats. There's standing up when people enter rooms. Instructions that feel more like ballroom choreography than relationship advice. And yes, there are assumptions about class, gender, and household roles that belong firmly to their era.

These moments don't diminish the book's value; they clarify it. Wisdom doesn't arrive in a vacuum. It comes dressed in the customs of its time. The outfit may go out of style, but the intention underneath often doesn't.

Reading these passages with good humor—rather than judgment—makes the experience richer. They show us not just how marriage was once imagined, but how carefully the author was trying to help men do better within the world he knew.

And if we're honest, one day our own blind spots will look just as quaint. Probably involving mobile phones.

A Final Word—from 1936, and from Us

Near the end of the book, the author reminds us that "the home is the one place where a man shows whether or not he is truly courteous." Anyone can be delightful in company. The harder test—and the more meaningful one—is how you behave with the people who see you every day and who know what you actually look like first thing in the morning.

That idea alone earns this book its place on a modern shelf.

We didn't republish *How to Be a Good Husband* to turn it into something it isn't. We brought it back because, beneath the social graces and the era's phrasing, it offers a clear-eyed, humane reminder of what actually holds marriages together.

We hope that you smiled more than you expected, paused for reflection a few times, and agreed with the book's

Closing Thoughts from The Husband School

message: marriage success isn't about perfection; it's about attention. The kind that shows up quietly, without applause, and builds a bond that can survive life's ups and downs.

Thanks for reading. And for trying to learn lessons from a classic 1930s marriage manual. That alone puts you ahead of most husbands—in any century.

About the Author

Rick Resnick is the founder and headmaster of The Husband School, a publisher focused on practical, relatable, and sometimes humorous guidance for men, regardless of marital status.

A longtime writer and former media executive, Rick has spent decades shaping editorial content and helping ideas connect with readers. In preparing this annotated edition of *How to Be a Good Husband*, his role was not to rewrite the original text, but to clarify it—highlighting what still resonates, providing context where necessary, pointing out some humor, and letting the book speak in its own voice.

Rick is also the author of *The New Husband's Survival Guide*, a modern companion to this volume that approaches marriage with a considerably lighter touch. (Many would say that it's laugh-out-loud funny.) Together, the two books reflect the belief that marriages are built less on grand gestures than on consideration, patience, and the small choices made every day.

When he's not writing or annotating vintage marriage manuals, Rick plays tennis and golf, obsessively supports Arsenal FC, and sings lead in a rock cover band. He lives in Pennsylvania with his wife, Carolyn, and their dog, Rocket.

Thank You for Reading

BEFORE YOU GO

You've reached the final page of a book first published in 1936, and hopefully discovered that some ideas about marriage age better than others.

If this annotated edition helped you see the original advice more clearly (or more humorously), a short review on your favorite book site can help other readers find it. A sentence or two is plenty.

If you'd like a more modern companion to this book, you might enjoy *The New Husband's Survival Guide*—a lighter, funnier, contemporary take on marriage from The Husband School.

You can learn more about upcoming projects and related books at:
www.husbandschool.co

And if you know someone who might appreciate a classic marriage manual (warts and all), passing this book along is encouraged.

With appreciation — Rick Resnick

The Husband School

www.husbandschool.co/contact

www.ingramcontent.com/pod-product-compliance
Lightning Source LLC
Chambersburg PA
CBHW050954050426
42337CB00051B/1090